As a birthday present for Sheila

Second Book of Descant Recorder Solos

Zweites Spielbuch für
Sopranblockflöte und Klavier

edited and arranged by

WALTER BERGMANN

Faber Music Limited
London

PREFACE

The purpose of this book is to widen the musical experience of the progressing recorder player.

It is essential that the pianist should master his part before joining the recorder player in ensemble.

The source of Nos. 5–8 is Telemann's *Der getreue Music-Meister;* Nos. 15–17 are from Haydn's so-called baryton trios which he composed for his employer, Prince Esterházy, and which contain a wealth of beautiful music. W.B.

VORWORT

Der Zweck dieses Buches ist, den musikalischen Ausblick des fortgeschrittenen Blockflötenspielers zu erweitern.

Es ist wichtig, dass der Pianist seine Stimme beherrscht, ehe er mit dem Blockflötenspieler zusammen spielt.

Die Vorlage für Nr. 5–8 ist Telemanns *Der getreue Music-Meister* und für Nr. 15–17 Haydns sogenannte Barytontrios, die er für seinen Brotherrn, Fürst Esterházy, komponierte und die eine Fülle der besten Musik enthalten. W.B.

© 1983 by Faber Music Ltd
First published in 1983 by Faber Music Ltd
3 Queen Square London WC1N 3AU
Music drawn by Sheila Stanton
Cover design by Shirley Tucker

Contents : Inhalt

1. Song
Lied

PHILIP ROSSETER
(1568–1623)

An Elizabethan love song.

Ein Elisabethanisches Liebeslied.

2. Prelude I

JOHANN SEBASTIAN BACH
(1685–1750)

The recorder and piano parts are of equal importance.
Blockflöten- und Pianostimme sind von gleicher Bedeutung.

3. Prelude II

JOHANN SEBASTIAN BACH
(1685–1750)

(Grave)

See note to No. 2.
Vgl. Anmerkung zu Nr. 2.

4. Andante

GEORGE FRIDERIC HANDEL
(1685–1759)

Andante indicates a moderate but forward-moving speed.
Andante erfordert ein mittelmässiges aber vorwärts strebendes Tempo.

5. Passepied

GEORG PHILIPP TELEMANN
(1681–1767)

A French dance in a slightly faster tempo than a minuet.
Ein französischer Tanz, etwas schneller als ein Menuett.

Da Capo al Fine

6. Pastourelle

GEORG PHILIPP TELEMANN
(1681–1767)

A tranquil shepherd's tune.
Eine ruhige Schäfermelodie.

7. Flauto Pastorale

GEORG PHILIPP TELEMANN
(1681 - 1767)

The title indicates a shepherd's pipe.
Flauto pastorale = Schäferpfeife.

8. Niaise

GEORG PHILIPP TELEMANN
(1681 – 1767)

A comic dance imitating a staggering (trainé) simpleton (niaise).
Ein komischer Tanz, der einen stolpernden (trainé) Einfaltspinsel (niaise) imitiert.

9. Gavotte

FRANCESCO BARSANTI
(1690-1772)

Barsanti, an Italian living in England, composed six important treble recorder sonatas. The gavotte and the minuet are taken from No. 3.

Barsanti, ein in England lebender Italiener, schrieb sechs bedeutende Altblockflötensonaten, von denen Nr. 3 die Gavotte und das Menuett enthält.

10. Minuet

FRANCESCO BARSANTI
(1690–1772)

See note to No. 9.
Vgl. Anmerkung zu Nr. 9.

11. Madge on the Tree *or* Margery Cree

English Country Dance
(1721)

12. Slater's Fancy

English Country Dance
(1719)

Play fast and slightly rough.
Spiel schnell und etwas derb

13. The Maiden's Blush *or* Bump her Belly

English Country Dance
(1719)

Fast and robust as the subtitle and bars 4 and 12 suggest.
Vgl. Nr. 12.

As a birthday present for Sheila

Second Book of Descant Recorder Solos

Zweites Spielbuch für
Sopranblockflöte und Klavier

edited and arranged by

WALTER BERGMANN

RECORDER PART

Faber Music Limited
London

© 1983 by Faber Music Ltd
First published in 1983 by Faber Music Ltd
3 Queen Square London WC1N 3AU
Music drawn by Sheila Stanton
Cover design by Shirley Tucker

Contents : Inhalt

PREFACE

The purpose of this book is to widen the musical experience of the progressing recorder player.

It is essential that the pianist should master his part before joining the recorder player in ensemble.

The source of Nos. 5-8 is Telemann's *Der getreue Music-Meister;* Nos. 15-17 are from Haydn's so-called baryton trios which he composed for his employer, Prince Esterházy, and which contain a wealth of beautiful music.   W.B.

VORWORT

Der Zweck dieses Buches ist, den musikalischen Ausblick des fortgeschrittenen Blockflötenspielers zu erweitern.

Es ist wichtig, dass der Pianist seine Stimme beherrscht, ehe er mit dem Blockflötenspieler zusammen spielt.

Die Vorlage für Nr. 5-8 ist Telemanns *Der getreue Music-Meister* und für Nr. 15-17 Haydns sogenannte Barytontrios, die er für seinen Brotherrn, Fürst Esterházy, komponierte und die eine Fülle der besten Musik enthalten.   W.B.

1. Song
Lied

PHILIP ROSSETER
(1568–1623)

Dolce

An Elizabethan love song.
Ein Elisabethanisches Liebeslied.

2. Prelude I

JOHANN SEBASTIAN BACH
(1685–1750)

(Andante)

The recorder and piano parts are of equal importance.

Blockflöten- und Pianostimme sind von gleicher Bedeutung.

3. Prelude II

JOHANN SEBASTIAN BACH
(1685-1750)

See note to No. 2.
Vgl. Anmerkung zu Nr. 2.

4. Andante

GEORGE FRIDERIC HANDEL
(1685-1759)

Andante indicates a moderate but forward-moving speed.
Andante erfordert ein mittelmässiges aber vorwärts strebendes Tempo.

5. Passepied

GEORG PHILIPP TELEMANN
(1681–1767)

Da Capo al Fine

A French dance in a slightly faster tempo than a minuet.
Ein französischer Tanz, etwas schneller als ein Menuett.

6. Pastourelle

GEORG PHILIPP TELEMANN
(1681–1767)

A tranquil shepherd's tune.
Eine ruhige Schäfermelodie.

7. Flauto Pastorale

GEORG PHILIPP TELEMANN
(1681–1767)

The title indicates a shepherd's pipe.
Flauto pastorale = Schäferpfeife.

8. Niaise

GEORG PHILIPP TELEMANN
(1681 - 1767)

A comic dance imitating a staggering (trainé) simpleton (niaise).
Ein komischer Tanz, der einen stolpernden (trainé) Einfaltspinsel (niaise) imitiert.

9. Gavotte

FRANCESCO BARSANTI
(1690–1772)

Barsanti, an Italian living in England, composed six important treble recorder sonatas.   The gavotte and the minuet are taken from No. 3.

Barsanti, ein in England lebender Italiener, schrieb sechs bedeutende Altblockflötensonaten, von denen Nr. 3 die Gavotte und das Menuett enthält.

10. Minuet

FRANCESCO BARSANTI
(1690–1772)

See note to No. 9.
Vgl. Anmerkung zu Nr. 9.

11. Madge on the Tree *or* Margery Cree

English Country Dance
(1721)

12. Slater's Fancy

English Country Dance
(1719)

Play fast and slightly rough.
Spiel schnell und etwas derb.

13. The Maiden's Blush *or* Bump her Belly

English Country Dance
(1719)

Fast and robust as the subtitle and bars 4 and 12 suggest.
Vgl. Nr. 12.

14. The Siege of Limerick
Die Belagerung von Limerick

English Country Dance
(1721)

The tune, a hornpipe, is actually by Henry Purcell.
Die Melodie, ein Hornpipe Tanz, stammt von Henry Purcell.

15. Partie: I Pastorale

JOSEPH HAYDN
(1732-1809)

Nos. 15, 16 and 17 can also be played as a unit.
Nrs. 15, 16 und 17 können auch als Einheit gespielt werden.

16. Partie: II Menuet

JOSEPH HAYDN
(1732–1809)

Menuet da Capo

See note to No. 15.
Vgl. Anmerkung zu Nr. 15.

17. Partie: III Finale

JOSEPH HAYDN
(1732–1809)

See note to No. 15.

Vgl. Anmerkung zu Nr. 15.

18. Pantomime

from the ballet 'Les Petits Riens'
aus dem Ballett 'Les Petits Riens'

WOLFGANG AMADEUS MOZART
(1756–1791)

19. Ländler I

FRANZ SCHUBERT
(1797–1828)

20. German Dance
Deutscher Tanz

FRANZ SCHUBERT
(1797–1828)

21. Ländler II

FRANZ SCHUBERT
(1797–1828)

22. Theme and Variations
Thema und Variationen

JOHANN ABRAHAM PETER SCHULZ
(1747–1800)

The theme is by Schulz; the variations are by the editor.
Das Thema ist von Schulz, für die Variationen ist der Herausgeber verantwortlich.

23. From the Album for the Young
Aus dem Album für die Jungend

ROBERT SCHUMANN Op. 68 no. 30
(1810-1856)

Without title.
Ohne Titel.

14. The Siege of Limerick
Die Belagerung von Limerick

English Country Dance
(1721)

The tune, a hornpipe, is actually by Henry Purcell.

Die Melodie, ein Hornpipe Tanz, stammt von Henry Purcell.

15. Partie: I Pastorale

JOSEPH HAYDN
(1732–1809)

Nos. 15, 16 and 17 can also be played as a unit.

Nrs. 15, 16 und 17 können auch als Einheit gespielt werden.

16. Partie: II Menuet

JOSEPH HAYDN
(1732–1809)

See note to No. 15.

Vgl. Anmerkung zu Nr. 15.

Menuet Da Capo

17. Partie: III Finale

JOSEPH HAYDN
(1732-1809)

See note to No. 15.
Vgl. Anmerkung zu Nr. 15.

18. Pantomime

from the ballet 'Les Petits Riens'
aus dem Ballett 'Les Petits Riens'

WOLFGANG AMADEUS MOZART
(1756-1791)

Da Capo al Fine

19. Ländler I

FRANZ SCHUBERT
(1797-1828)

20. German Dance
Deutscher Tanz

FRANZ SCHUBERT
(1797-1828)

21. Ländler II

FRANZ SCHUBERT
(1797-1828)

22. Theme and Variations
Thema und Variationen

JOHANN ABRAHAM PETER SCHULZ
(1747-1800)

The theme is by Schulz; the variations are by the editor.
Das Thema ist von Schulz, für die Variationen ist der Herausgeber verantwortlich.

Var.1 Un poco meno mosso

Var.2 Allegro moderato

Var. 3 Sostenuto

Il Tema Da Capo

23. From the Album for the Young

Aus dem Album für die Jungend

ROBERT SCHUMANN Op. 68 no. 30
(1810-1856)

Slow, with deep expression

Without title.
Ohne Titel.

RECORDER MUSIC
from Faber Music

WALTER BERGMANN

First Book of Treble Solos
ISBN 0-571-50546-5

First Book of Descant Solos
ISBN 0-571-50587-2

Second Book of Descant Solos
ISBN 0-571-50676-3

BRIAN BONSOR

Play Country Dances
ISBN 0-571-51004-3

The Really Easy Recorder Book
ISBN 0-571-51037-X

PAUL HARRIS

Improve your sight-reading! Descant Recorder Grades 1–3
ISBN 0-571-51373-5

MARLENE HOBSBAWM

Me and My Recorder Part 1
ISBN 0-571-51045-0

Me and My Recorder Part 2
ISBN 0-571-51052-3

ANDREW LLOYD WEBBER

Cats Selection (recorder duet and piano)
ISBN 0-571-50905-3

PAM WEDGWOOD

RecorderWorld – Very first adventures in recorder playing
Book 1: ISBN 0-571-51985-7   Book 2: ISBN 0-571-52239-4
Teacher's Book: ISBN 0-571-51984-9   Accompaniment CD: 0-571-52290-4

FABER *ff* MUSIC